Toxic

Toxic

A Tour of the Ecuadorian Amazon

Amelia Fiske and Jonas Fischer

UNIVERSITY OF TORONTO PRESS
Toronto Buffalo London

Toronto Buffalo London
utorontopress.com
Printed in Canada

ISBN 978-1-4875-0951-4 (cloth)
ISBN 978-1-4875-0952-1 (paper)
ISBN 978-1-4875-0954-5 (EPUB)
ISBN 978-1-4875-0953-8 (PDF)

Library and Archives Canada Cataloguing in Publication

Title: Toxic : a tour of the Ecuadorian Amazon / Amelia Fiske and Jonas Fischer.
Names: Fiske, Amelia, author. | Fischer, Jonas (Artist), artist.
Description: Series statement: EthnoGRAPHIC | Includes bibliographical references.
Identifiers: Canadiana (print) 20230562094 | Canadiana (ebook) 20230562124 | ISBN 9781487509521 (paper) | ISBN 9781487509514 (cloth) | ISBN 9781487509538 (PDF) | ISBN 9781487509545 (EPUB)
Subjects: LCSH: Petroleum industry and trade – Environmental aspects – Ecuador – Comic books, strips, etc. | LCSH: Petroleum industry and trade – Social aspects – Ecuador – Comic books, strips, etc. | LCSH: Pollutants – Ecuador – Comic books, strips, etc. | LCSH: Ecuador – Environmental conditions – Comic books, strips, etc. | LCSH: Ecuador – Tours – Comic books, strips, etc. | LCGFT: Comics (Graphic works)
Classification: LCC HD9574.E22 F57 2024 | DDC 338.2/728209866 – dc23

Cover design: John Beadle
Cover image: Jonas Fischer

We welcome comments and suggestions regarding any aspect of our publications – please feel free to contact us at news@utorontopress.com or visit us at utorontopress.com.

Every effort has been made to contact copyright holders; in the event of an error or omission, please notify the publisher.

We wish to acknowledge the land on which the University of Toronto Press operates. This land is the traditional territory of the Wendat, the Anishnaabeg, the Haudenosaunee, the Métis, and the Mississaugas of the Credit First Nation.

University of Toronto Press acknowledges the financial support of the Government of Canada and the Ontario Arts Council, an agency of the Government of Ontario, for its publishing activities.

Funded by the Government of Canada | Financé par le gouvernement du Canada | Canada

For Donald and Leonela

Contents

Introduction

We are living in an era of toxicity. Oil and its many derivatives surround us. As one of the principal drivers of anthropogenic change, oil production has rapidly transformed how life is lived around the globe. Lago Agrio and the surrounding areas of the Ecuadorian Amazon are a prime example of the present predicament: the very petrochemical compounds that sustain our lives today also produce tremendous harm.

One of the principal ways that people who do not live in this area of the Amazon come to know about the realities of oil contamination has been through toxic tours. Donald Moncayo, a leading environmental activist in the region, has been giving these tours for students, lawyers, journalists, foreign tourists, and local individuals for years. In the toxic tours, Donald enrolls participants as witnesses to the realities of life alongside oil operations. Participants listen to the squeak of the hand auger as contaminated soil is pulled from the ground, they feel the squish of oily leaves between their fingers, they hold their noses against the fumes of the gas flares overhead. As the tour winds through the provinces of Sucumbíos and Orellana, the participants meet other residents who share with them their stories of struggle, loss, and life in the region. Along the way, Donald recounts a deeply personal history woven within these industrial legacies. The toxic tours contextualize local harm, making individual stories and chemical encounters speak to broader histories of oil extraction and linking it to systems of consumption and injustice that may not otherwise be immediately visible.

Toxic gives life to one focus of my anthropological field research, which was conducted between 2011 and 2013. Throughout this time, I lived in Lago Agrio, the city that marks the site of the first wells drilled by the Texaco Company in Ecuador in the 1960s. I observed how the toxicants used and produced in oil production cross boundaries, breaching the industrial membranes installed to contain the contents of waste pits, spills, and the effects of industry more broadly. While official accounts insist that harm from oil is controlled with advanced technology, everyday life in the region – such as the experiences afforded through the toxic tour – contests such claims. As a focus of my ethnographic fieldwork, I went on dozens of tours with Donald, intrigued by the ways that he wove together complicated histories of oil production, technical questions of regulation and legislation, and the deeply personal accounts of loss and suffering of the people who live alongside this industry. While I have written about this work in other academic forums (Fiske 2018; 2020a; 2020b; 2023), Jonas Fischer's visual rendering of the tour in this story brings Donald's work to life differently. It allows for experimentation with the sensory aspects of contamination, toxicity, and loss that exceed narrative description. This book is an invitation for readers to travel along on a toxic tour with the participants in the story.

Toxic takes readers on a tour over the course of one day. The book is not intended to be an account of any one particular tour that I attended, but rather draws from many in order to convey the experience of a toxic tour. Throughout I have drawn on Donald's narrations of the tours that were recorded in my fieldnotes. However, Jonas and I have also taken liberties to change, add, combine, or condense different parts of this narration, and as such it should not be taken as a verbatim reporting of his words. Leonela, Donald's daughter, is included in the story with his permission. She was a toddler when I conducted research for this project and often accompanied her father on his toxic tours. When I returned in 2020, I learned that she is now an activist in her own right: Leonela has led her friends and classmates in initiating a lawsuit against the state for the ongoing burning of gas from the flares in the region, which are a continual threat to people's health and children's health in particular. In this story, she is depicted as a little girl around five years old. Her character is thus a fictional creation inspired by Leonela's accompaniment of her father's tours and her own activism as she grew older. I have created the other characters based on people I met while conducting fieldwork; some of these characters are composites, some draw more heavily from the biographies of particular individuals and their recorded remarks during my fieldwork. All should ultimately be understood as fictional representations informed by ethnographic research. The story recounted here is drawn directly from my fieldwork; however, we have used the graphic medium to intentionally engage with sensory and metaphorical elements of encounters with toxicity.

During a research stay at the Rachel Carson Center for Environment and Society at the Ludwig Maximilian University of Munich in 2017, a conversation with Amy Moran Thomas provided the necessary spark for me to pursue this project. Initially, Jonas and I started working on a pilot project, a graphic article entitled "Toxic

Inheritance," which we subsequently published with *The Nib* (2020). An Engaged Anthropology grant from the Wenner-Gren Foundation allowed Jonas and I to travel to Ecuador in February 2020, during which we shared "Toxic Inheritance" at the Humboldt Association in Quito and the Amisacho Foundation in Lago Agrio. While there we hosted public forums to debate the role of toxicity in everyday life, along with a workshop for people living in the Amazon on the use of graphic art for activism and popular education. This trip was critical in the development of this book. It enabled Jonas to spend time in Ecuador, to meet Donald and go on several days of a toxic tour for himself, and to spend time in Lago Agrio. It was also a chance for me to return to a place where I had lived for more than two years and contemplate what it would mean for Lago Agrio to be "post-oil" – a remark made by Donald on this visit while reflecting on the changes in the region. Upon our return to Germany, we began working on the script for this book, which we completed over the rest of the following year.

My debts are many in the making of this book. The ethnographic research for this book was made possible by the Social Science Research Council, Wenner-Gren Foundation, National Science Foundation, UNC Graduate School, and the UNC Institute for Study of the Americas. I am grateful for the guidance of my doctoral committee at the University of North Carolina at Chapel Hill in the development of the research that informed this graphic novel. Thank you to Margaret Wiener, Peter Redfield, Rudi Colloredo-Mansfeld, Barry Saunders, and Michele Rivkin-Fish. Friends and colleagues read drafts of the script and provided feedback along the way; I am grateful to Katinka Hakuta, Brittany Peats, Lucy Sommo, Dragana Lassiter, and Carson Fiske for their keen eyes and support.

Many people in Ecuador have been significant in the development of this project, from fieldwork to the making of this graphic novel. Donald Moncayo was endlessly generous with his time and knowledge, answering my questions and letting me tag along on tour after tour. I hope that this book captures some of the virtue and spirit with which he dedicates himself to making the Amazon a better place for all to live in. Many other individuals in Ecuador made this research possible, and lifted my spirits along the way. I am grateful for Kati and Sebastián Álvarez, Enrique Novas, Santiago del Hierro, Vanessita Roa, Lexie Gropper, José Luis Muñoz, Mitch Anderson, Jorge Mideros, Shaila Carvajal, Mariana Jimenez, Manuel Pallares, Pablo Fajardo, Alba Gonzaga, Liber Macias, Beatriz Romero, Alfredo López, Luz Arpi, Esteban Salazar, Elizabeth Bastidias, Diego Róman, Alex Báez, Marie-Pierre Smets, and Lindsay Ofrias for each of their contributions to this process.

Carli Hansen at the University of Toronto Press has overseen the progress of this project and helped Jonas and I to navigate specific challenges along the way. I thank the three anonymous reviewers who helped to improve the book through peer review. Mike Cepek has been an enthusiastic supporter and provided important feedback during revisions of the text. In my postdoctoral work, I am indebted to the support of Alena Buyx at the Technical University of Munich, from whom I have learned so much over the past six years. Colleagues from the TUM have also supported this process, in particular Stuart McLennan and Jennifer Wladarsch. In Kiel, both Jonas and I have benefitted greatly from the keen guidance of Markus Huber at the Mutheisus School of Fine Arts since the very beginning of this project as a graphic article. Ronald Gutberlet generously assisted us with the crafting of the script. I am so grateful to everyone who has helped this story move from an idea to the book you hold in your hands.

Finally, I would like to thank my family near and far for their continued love and support: Patty Sheehan and Richard Fiske, Carson Fiske and his family – Becky Colman, Zachary Fiske, and Ainsley Fiske – and in particular to Andrea Ricci and our dearest Livia and Alba. Working with Jonas has been a serendipitous collaboration from the start. I am ever grateful to have had the chance to collaborate on a subject that is so dear to my heart, with someone who has taken it on as their own and given it new life with their creative intuition. I hope that you all, as readers, will each find your own connections to this story as we each contemplate what comes next when living in a toxic world.

Amelia Fiske
Kiel, Germany

While completing my MA thesis, this book was the subject of many weekly feedback sessions with Markus Huber, my professor at the Muthesius University of Fine Arts and Design. I cherish the conversations and discussions about all the moving parts that making a graphic novel of this scale entails, but also the conversations where there were no new drawings, storylines, or technical questions to discuss but all the more things to talk about. I have so much to thank him for and I am most grateful to have studied with him.

I want to thank my friends, art school and Ateliergemeinschaft studiomates: Louise, Milan, Torben, Katya, Leonie, Mateusz, Neele, Leo, Sören, Lina, Anna, Viktor, Monika, Hanna, Jonas, Benni, André, Timo, Justus, Kaspar, and Niko. They were always around for artistic feedback and, equally important, smoke breaks, chitchats, coffee runs, canteen lunches, ranting about campus politics, quick walks around the park, coins for the vending machine. I thank them for sharing their makings, insights, and thoughts, for their support during my MA thesis, and for their company. A special thanks to Leo, who, besides being a steady support throughout, made my handwriting come to life as a digital font through a meticulous process. I also want to thank Carli Hansen, Christoph Schuler, and Ronald Gutberlet for their support, help, and encouragement.

I'd like to thank all the generous and kind people that Amelia and I met on our trip to Ecuador: Enrique Novas from Casa Humboldt/Goethe Institute Quito, Lexi Gropper from Amisacho, the six Norwegian guys who let me tag along on their private bus tour for a bit, and, most importantly, Donald Moncayo for letting us turn Amelia's observations of his toxic tours into sequential art.

While working on this book – from our collaboration that preceded it and certainly everything that will follow – I have learned so much from Amelia. Thank you for letting me be an equal part in this; I consider myself very lucky to be working with you. I couldn't have wished for a better partner in this project.

My friend Louise always says that the sketch is often better than the drawing. Consequently, in an effort to obtain graphic novel pages that possess the spontaneity, ease, and clear expression of a sketch, I skipped the sketching stage and instead went straight to pen and ink on plain paper, trusting my line, and trying to follow its lead. Many of the drawings are paste-overs with second, third, sometimes even fourth attempts and a whole lot of rogue lines – remnants of my line approximating the right form. I let a lot of these traces survive the process of digitally cleaning, collaging, and rearranging the scans prior to adding color. I hope that the readers will enjoy these suggestions of the process that led to this book.

Jonas Fischer
Kiel, Germany

Tour Participants

Donald Moncayo is the son of settlers from Loja who arrived in Lago Agrio in the 1970s. He grew up in the Lago Agrio oil camp. Following the deaths of his parents, at an early age he took over responsibility for the family farm with his siblings and saw how disputes over land, jobs, and contamination divided communities affected by oil drilling. As a young adult, he was witness to a negotiation between a neighbor and an oil company representative following a spill on the neighbor's farm. The neighbor's chickens had drunk contaminated water and were close to death. The oil company representative told the property owner that he wouldn't reimburse the loss of the chickens because they weren't dead yet. The moment changed Donald's life and, filled with indignation, he began to see the widespread injustice driven by the industry that he had grown up with in a new light. Over the past two decades, he has become a leading environmental activist in the area, joining forces with the Frente de Defensa de la Amazonía, and then with the Union of People Affected by Texaco. He is known for his expertise in giving toxic tours for visitors to the region, through which he continues to fight for justice for the Amazon.

Leonela (Leo) is Donald's daughter and loves to accompany her father on toxic tours. Watching her father's work has informed her own perspective growing up in the region, cultivating her keen sense of environmental activism from a young age.

Elena is a young woman from just outside of Guayaquil, a large port city in Ecuador located on the banks of the Guayas River leading to the Pacific Ocean. Although the Ecuadorian economy depends in a significant part on oil revenue, and Elena has heard her parents and aunts and uncles describe their memories of the oil boom in the 1970s, she has never seen the industry firsthand. While studying at the University of Guayaquil, she made friends with people who were involved in environmental activism. They organized campaigns to collect signatures for initiatives like the Yasuní-ITT, a movement to keep oil in the soil in the Amazon, and she became increasingly interested in alternative forms of development. She has big, romantic ideas about what the Amazon is like but has never been there. After the toxic tour, she is heading further east, following a long-time dream of swimming with pink dolphins in the Cuyabeno Wildlife Reserve.

Angela lives in Richmond, California, in a neighborhood on the outskirts of the Chevron refinery, which was originally built by Standard Oil. She and her neighbors have been suffering from health problems that they believe are related to the refinery, including persistent headaches and trouble breathing when the refinery fumes blow in their direction. For the past several years she has begun to organize with other community members, sometimes working on "bucket brigades" to measure air quality in different parts of the city. Other times, she can be found protesting in front of Chevron offices to commemorate the anniversary of a refinery explosion that covered Richmond in black clouds of toxic smoke in 2012. After watching Ecuadorian activists protesting at a Chevron shareholders meeting, she decided to travel to Ecuador to see things for herself. Given her own experiences living outside the Chevron refinery, what she encounters on this toxic tour is deeply personal.

Gianluca recently finished a degree in development studies and took a position with Oxfam Italia, an aid organization dedicated to fighting inequality and ending poverty around the world. He has been living in Lago Agrio for almost two years, working on food security issues in Sucumbíos province along the border between Ecuador and Colombia. He spends his days conducting outreach visits in communities, holding workshops, and organizing distribution networks from the Lago Agrio office. He's easily spotted as a foreign aid worker with his telltale blue vest and scooter, and he spends his free time with others from the extensive foreign aid community in the city. Up to this point, he had been so focused on issues of food security and border violence that he had yet to contemplate the relationships between oil development and other forms of social inequality. As a pragmatist and a bit of a skeptic, Gianluca is always looking for ways to fix problems that he encounters in his travels.

Oil Contamination

Oil is made from decaying biomass caught between layers of sedimentary rock for millions of years. In the drilling process, the underground slurry is extracted and separated into crude oil, natural gas, and formation waters, which are then refined to produce diesel fuel, gasoline, jet fuel, asphalt, and thousands of other derivative products, such as plastics, medical supplies, pesticides, paint, and more. While oil is one product of extraction that can be processed and sold, formation water and the chemicals that are added during the drilling process must be discarded. In the early years of oil operations in Ecuador, formation and production waters were dumped into waste pits or sometimes left to run directly into streams and the surrounding environment. Today, these waste waters are usually reinjected underground through converted oil wells.

Another product of oil extraction is gas. In Ecuador, these combustible vapors generated in extraction are burned in gas flares, most often near production stations or wells. As a result, the areas near the flares are covered in fine toxic particulate matter. People who live close to the flares report problems with toxic rain. The flares do not always operate properly, and they emit methane and volatile organic compounds like sulfur dioxide. Aromatic hydrocarbons such as benzene, toluene, and xylene (BTX) are also released. During consortium operations, approximately three waste pits were built with each well. In the *Aguinda* lawsuit, 880 pits were verified, each approximately sixty by forty meters (200 x 130 feet) in size and two meters (6.5 feet) deep, carved out of the ground like large swimming pools. As operations went on, new waste pits were dug, such that sometimes one well might have six or seven pits. Waste pits were not lined, creating a substantial risk of contamination of the surrounding soil and groundwater.

A pipe, often called the gooseneck (*cuello de ganso*) pipe, was a common design element of consortium operations. One end of the pipe sat in the pit above the surface, and the other end of the pipe protruded from the outer bank of the pit. Given the frequent rains in the Amazon that would collect on top of the waste pits, the pipe was installed in order to allow excess water to drain and thus prevent the pits from overflowing. In practice, the gooseneck pipe allowed the contents of the waste pits, including rainwater that contained toxic chemicals, to drain into the surrounding environment without any treatment. Waste pits with gooseneck pipes were in place for decades and can still be found throughout the region.

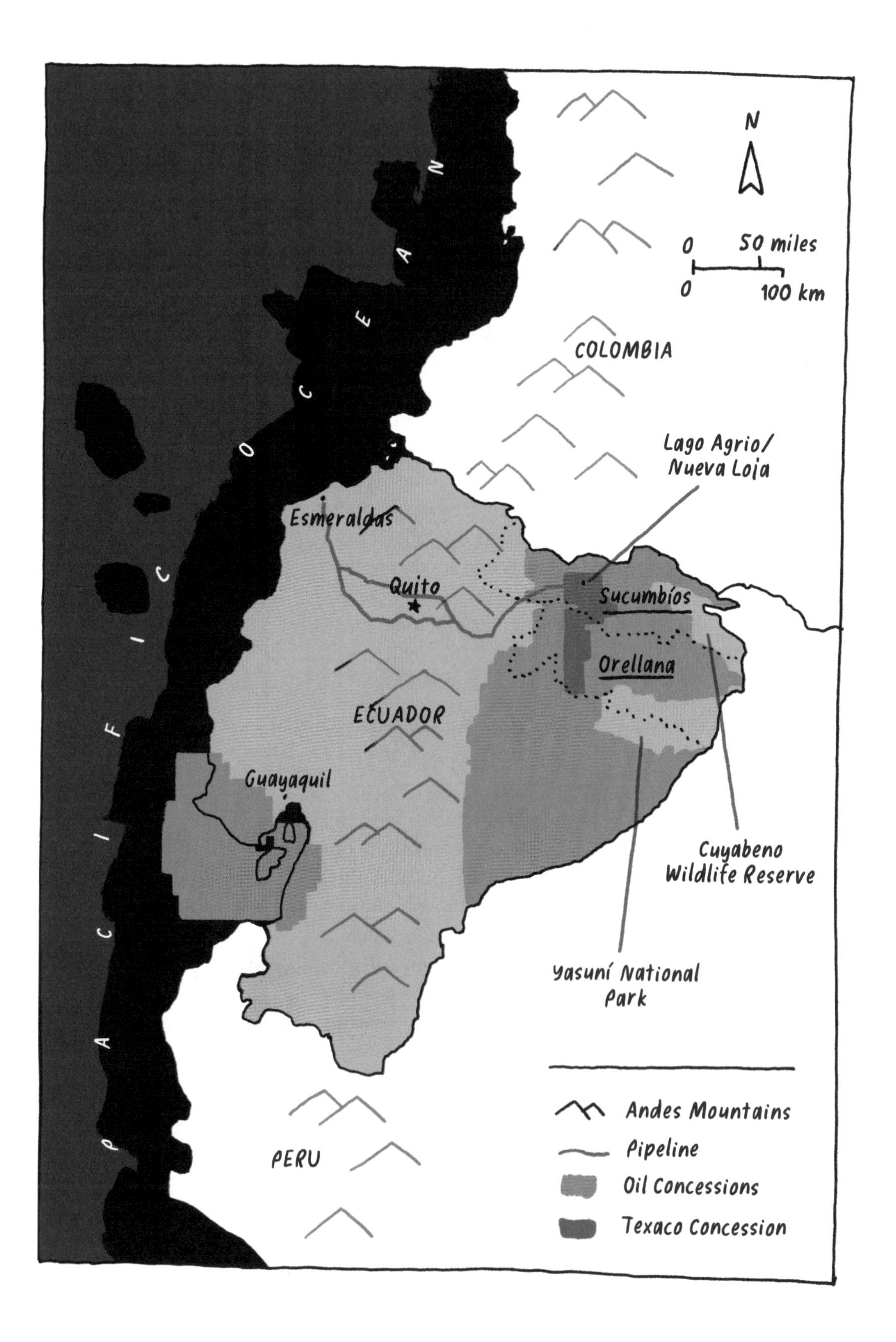

N
0 50 miles
0 100 km
COLOMBIA
PACIFIC OCEAN
Lago Agrio/
Nueva Loja
Esmeraldas
Quito
Sucumbíos
Orellana
ECUADOR
Guayaquil
Cuyabeno
Wildlife Reserve
Yasuní National
Park
PERU
Andes Mountains
Pipeline
Oil Concessions
Texaco Concession

Beginnings

Señores y señoras...
We are starting our descent into Lago Agrio.

Please bring your seat into an upright and locked position and open the window blinds.

Please remain seated until the captain has switched off the seatbelt sign.

CRUDE-2009
THE REAL PRICE OF OIL

Welcome to Lago Agrio. The temperature is currently 33° Celsius, and the local time is 5:28pm.

is town pulses wit
e life of the oil industr
chaotic market, dusty
reets, thick traffic and
ritty bars. The first oil
vorkers nicknamed La
Agrio 'bitter lake,' afte
Sour Lake, Texas, the
former home of Texa
which pioneered loca
The city's off

Bzzz
Bzzz

Hola Mamá...
Sí...
Yes, we're almost there, I think.

Right? I'm so excited. I can't wait to see the jungle.
What?
Yes, of course I'll be careful.

Yes, Mamá, I'm old enough, I'll manage.
I'll text you when I'm at the hotel.
Yes. Love you, bye.

Gianluca

Hola!

Hey hermano! How's it going?
Not too bad.
How is the San Antonio community?

Doing a bit better than before, I'd say.
But you know... it's hard.
I'm about to finish up their shipment for tomorrow.

Oh--
--Señora Lopez was looking for you the other day.

Ah yes, I've been meaning to check on her.
Thanks for letting me know.

I won't be coming in tomorrow, I'm going on a toxic tour.
With Donald?

You know him?
Yes, we went to school together.
Give him my best, will you?

BANC
Buen provecho!
Gracias.

Good morning, Papá.

Good morning, my love. No school today?
No, my teacher is sick.

Do you have a tour today?
yes.

Ooohh, let me guess who is going. If I guess right, can I come?
Sure.
Is it schoolkids?
No
Hmmm... Germans?
Not today, tomorrow is with the Germans.
Americans?
Yes, one. Along with someone from Italy and a woman from Guayaquil.
Guayaquil! Where Mamá is from!
Exactly, where your grandmother lives.

LAGO AGRIO

SHARE
Arrived in Lago Agrio last night. Headed out on a toxic tour today. Can't wait to share this experience! #ecuador #toxictour
Excuse me...

Is this seat taken?

No, please, take a seat.
Thanks!

I didn't expect this place to be so full for breakfast.

Hi, I'm Elena.
Nice to meet you, I'm Angela.
Where are you from?
I'm from Richmond, California, in the United States.

So, what are you doing in Lago? Are you here to take a jungle trip?
In Ecuador there are just so many beautiful places to visit.

Well, kind of. I'm going on a tour today to see all the oil production in the jungle.

Is the tour with Donald? The toxic tour? I'm going too!

Oh, that's wonderful. It's so nice to meet you.
Are you excited?
Oh yes!

Señora.
Gracias.

Here you go.
Thanks.
Gosh, that is a lot of food!
I know!

Look at all this food -- plantains, rice, eggs, beans.
The sign says it's the "oil worker special." I guess we will be ready for a long day.

You know, I'm very interested to learn more about the environmental activism that's going on here.
Where I live in Richmond, there's a large Chevron refinery very close to my home.

My neighbors and I, we are working to improve the air quality for communities like ours that live next to the refinery.

Wow, it's great that you came all the way here.
I have to say, I'm from Ecuador but I have no idea what to expect. A friend talked me into going on the tour.

It's my first time in the Amazon. I've always dreamed of visiting the Cuyabeno.

Your first time? But you're from here?
Well yes, but I live in Guayaquil on the Pacific coast. So I've never been to the east, what they call El Oriente.
Fair enough. I live in the US and haven't been to the Grand Canyon...

Hi.

Are you guys also here for the tour?

Hi.
Yes we are. Have a seat, Donald said he'd be here at nine.
Do you want a coffee?

Thanks, but I'm fine. I had some at home.
You know, Italians – we're a bit picky about coffee.

I'm Gianluca by the way. Nice to meet you.
I'm Angela.

Is that scooter rented, or do you live here?
Hi, Elena.
My pleasure.

Well, at the moment I do.
I've been here for the past year and a half. I'm originally from Lecce, in southern Italy.

But for the past few years I've been working for Oxfam Italia on food security issues.
That's what brought me to Ecuador.

So you work here in Lago?
Well, the headquarters for the region is here but we serve communities all over Sucumbíos.

Can I bring you anything, sir?
No, thanks.

There are a lot of communities that live in very precarious conditions.
Some places don't have running water.
Gracias.

We serve many refugee families, and many of them don't have reliable access to food.
Wow, that sounds like important work! Do these people live near the oil operations?

Well...
A lot of communities have active operations, and nearly everyone lives in proximity to some sort of oil infrastructure.
Oil is just ubiquitous here.
But I have to say, despite oil being everywhere and hearing people speak about spills every now and then--
--I don't really know all that much about it.
So that's why I'm here today.

That's interesting! I would have thought that everyone here already knew about this.
Well, not me.
I've just been too busy to go on a tour until now...
HONK
Buenos días!

I'm Donald Moncayo, with the Union of People Affected by Texaco Oil Operations.
I'll be your guide today for the toxic tour. Welcome to Lago Agrio!
Mucho gusto.
This is my assistant, Leonela.
Hi Leonela!

Do you help your dad often with the toxic tours?
She's always a big help when she comes along. Right, Leo?
It might seem like she's shy now, but just wait...

Legacies

So, welcome to your first toxic tour.
Today I'm going to take you around to some sites where you can experience what the oil industry has done to this beautiful place for yourself.
Feel free to ask me any questions you have along the way.
To your left you can see the Petroecuador station. It was built at the beginning of the oil boom. Those tanks hold many, many barrels of crude.

I saw these tanks from the plane. It's all right here in the city!
Yes, but when oil exploration started the city wasn't here. Actually, the oil companies didn't want the settlers to build here.
But as more and more people started coming, the city and the industry grew together.

So, Donald, are you from the area?
Esteban, a colleague of mine, says he went to school with you.

You work at Oxfam with him, right? How is he?
He's doing alright. We work together in the warehouse.

And yes, I grew up here.
My parents were settlers. My father arrived in the second group of colonists in the 1970s.

Then my mother came two years later.
They met here.

I was born about a year later. Some 200 meters away from the Lago-2 well. So you could say I really am from here.
I was born in relation to the oil operations, watching them everyday.
So, I guess you have seen how much this place has been transformed?
I'd say so.

We've seen so many changes over the years--
--from back in the days when the companies could just do whatever they wanted, to the largest environmental class action lawsuit in the world.
You see the pipelines over there? They follow all the roads here. Or, rather, the roads follow them...

I remember walking along here on my way to school.
My brothers and sister and I would walk on top of the pipeline in order to avoid the roads, which had been covered in sticky crude to keep the dust down.
That way, when we arrived at school, our shoes wouldn't be ruined.

Hey, I like your shoes...
Thanks.
They're new.

Where are you from?
I'm from a town near Guayaquil.

Do you know where that is? It's on the Pacific coast.
Oh, I know where that is. I've even been there before.

Wow, look at that gas flare!
...

Do you not have oil where you are from?
Hmm?

Well, no, not really. I've never seen any of this before, no oil wells, no storage tanks...
Actually, I came here because I've always dreamed of seeing the Cuyabeno.

I also want to go down the Aguarico River all the way to the Peruvian Border--
-- and I'm really hoping to see some monkeys.

We have howler monkeys here!
My dad and I saw some the other day! A whole family was up in a tree.
Wow, I'd love to see howlers!

My trip to the Cuyabeno doesn't start until tomorrow. So a friend recommended that I go on one of these tours with your dad on my free day.
Sometimes, like today, I help him with the tour.

I'm sure he likes having you along.
Soon you'll be able to give your own tours!

Who was here first? The oil companies or the farmers?
...

Well, actually the Indigenous nationalities were here first--

-- but then people from all over Ecuador came here looking for land.

This was during the time that oil exploration was occurring.

The government had promised people 50 hectares of land each as long as they would farm it.
So people came to claim their farms, following the roads that were opened up by the oil companies who were building more and more wells here.
That's why these roads seem to follow the pipelines, because each one leads to a different well.

The settlers came and started their farms, brought in cattle and chickens and planted cacao.

They soon opened up second rows of farms along the roads.
This was a political project called Agrarian Reform.

Some settlers came a bit later, after oil development was already underway.

They found nice flat spots next to the well platforms--
--and they thought, "this would be a great place to build a house."

And then later, once they had built their houses, they found out that underneath there were waste pits--
--that had been covered over by the oil companies.

Like the Sánchez family, Papá?
Yes.
The company just covered them over with some dirt. Same technique as a cat.
No offense to cats, of course. I don't want to insult them by comparing them to Texaco.

So, in the 1960s the Ecuadorian State joined with the Texaco and Gulf Companies of the United States to create a consortium.
But because the newly formed state company, CEPE, did not know anything about extracting oil, Texaco managed the operations.

In 1967, oil extraction started here at the Lago Agrio-1 well. It is now inactive.
Over the next 20 years, they drilled 339 wells like this one and also built 18 production stations, extracting around 1.5 billion barrels of crude.
There was also a lot of oil that was just spilled into streams--
--and production waters that were dumped into waste pits--
--and waste pits that were lit on fire when they were full.

What are production waters?

So, when crude oil is in the ground it is mixed with formation water and gas.
When they bring it up to the surface, they have to separate it into the three components.

Radioactive materials and other chemicals are added during the drilling process, resulting in production waters.
They are highly toxic and are one of the worst byproducts of extraction.
They disperse easily into land and water.

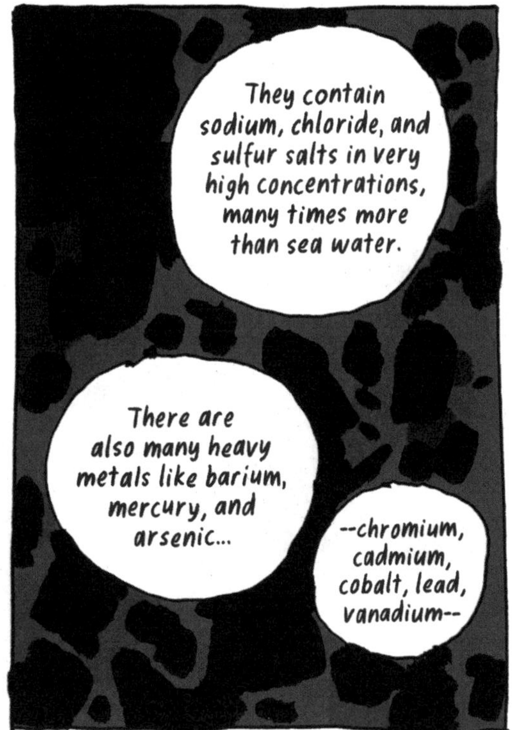
They contain sodium, chloride, and sulfur salts in very high concentrations, many times more than sea water.
There are also many heavy metals like barium, mercury, and arsenic...
--chromium, cadmium, cobalt, lead, vanadium--

--and of course hydrocarbons like benzopyrene, which is extremely carcinogenic.
Imagine all of that just running into the ground...

Well, matter of fa--
Hooo! Compa!

Papá?

Why is Don Gonzalo carrying all that water?
Because of the spill on his farm from last week.

Spill?
Oh yeah, we get a lot of spills here.
It's still a problem to find clean water for many of my neighbors.
So Don Gonzalo has to go into town and bring water home so that they can cook because now their well water is not safe for drinking, or cooking, or just about anything.

But shouldn't somebody come and clean it up?

Oh, the environmental authorities already came by to take a look and put in booms to contain the spill.

But it will be a long time before Don Gonzalo wants to drink his water again.

You know, some people around here--
--they have to drink the water anyways, despite it smelling like gasoline.

That's terrible!
And sometimes --
--like when chickens drink bad water--
--with oil in it--
--they dance around like crazy before they die.
Right, Papá?
That's the sad truth, dear.

You know--

--the other day someone from a community we work with told me about how sometimes they go to fish in the nearby river.

And when they cut open the fish they smell of oil.

I thought it must be some kind of jungle myth.
I mean --
-- maybe it was like that in the past, but things must be better now, right?

Unfortunately, that is the reality that we are living. Fish, capybaras, you name it.

Look, there's Don Gonzalo's Farm. I'll just make a quick stop here.

How are you guys doing? It's really a lot to take in.

I'm fine
-- I think.
All of this will probably take some time to sink in.

Same.
I mean, I've gotten so used to seeing oil pipelines everywhere but--
--learning about the scale of pollution is heavy.
W-what about you, Angela?

Well...
Where I live there's also a lot of oil production.
It's awful to see the same story here.

Seeing what was done to the people here is heartbreaking.
But the ways Donald and others support their communities is also very empowering.

You see, this is what's happening here...
All these pipeline spills--
--just last week a truck carrying formation waters tipped over in Taracoa.

The entire area was contaminated.
...
How are people supposed to live like this?

I can't believe that this just happens like this...
Yes, and far more often than you'd think.

It's just...
Well, how is this possible?

So--
--on my way to Ecuador I watched the documentary "CRUDE" about the big lawsuit here.
Is that still going on?
Ah yes, the Aguinda v. Texaco case.

In 1993, a lawsuit was filed on behalf of 30,000 people from here against Texaco.

It was for harm that had been done to the environment and to the health of those of us who lived here during the operations of the consortium.
This was a really big lawsuit.
After a long struggle in the U.S. and then later in Ecuador, the court here in Lago Agrio finally found Chevron guilty.

Guilty of negligence and extensive contamination.
Wait.
I thought it was Texaco that operated here?

They did!
But then Chevron bought Texaco in a merger in 2001.
And since then, Chevron has tried to say that they aren't responsible for the things that Texaco did in Ecuador.

However, Judge Zambrano found Chevron guilty and fined them $9.5 billion.
But we haven't seen a single cent yet.
You know, the Chevron CEO said that they'd fight until hell freezes over and then some.

Bastards!

Honestly. What a disgrace.

This is the kind of thing you see with oil companies all the time.
Whether here in Ecuador, or in communities in the U.S.

They seem to act like the lives of poor people and people of color don't matter.

It certainly seems that way...

So, we have to cross the Aguarico River now.
I hope you all brought your bathing suits?

Welcome to the Jenny Napali, our trusty barge with premium views of the river.

Hey Donald!

How's it going?
WROOOM

Good, good.
I'm taking these folks to the Aguarico-4 well for a toxic tour.
Ah, great.

This is my friend Jhony, come say hi.

Hi guys, nice to meet you.
I'm glad you've come to see what oil has done to our territory.

Territory?
Yes, this is Cofán territory.

That's right.
Lago Agrio, where we were before, that was ancestral Cofán land when Texaco arrived.

Mhm
The Cofán used the forest for hunting.
The rivers were clean.

My parents and grandparents used the rivers to travel and fish and bathe.

But then everything changed because of oil.

My uncle Emeregildo, he's a Cofán elder--
--and sometimes works with Donald doing toxic tours.

He was a child when Texaco arrived.
He remembers these loud contraptions flying over the forest.
They had never seen anything like it, they thought they were big metal birds.

Helicopters!

Yes, exactly.

Then they noticed this strange black stuff in the water floating downstream.

One day they decided to find out where all this was coming from--

--they followed it upstream and arrived at the place that is now the Lago Agrio-1 well.
Maybe you saw it on your tour?
Yes, we were there earlier this morning...

Well...
You have to remember that back then, things weren't built up like they are now.
There was no city.
Lago Agrio-1 was a huge 10-hectare plot in the middle of the forest that had been cleared for the company.
When Emeregildo and his family arrived, the Texaco workers gave them some gifts--
Gifts?

They gave them diesel, panela, and cheese.
Emeregildo's parents didn't know what these things were so they took them to the missionaries.
VRRR

They came and polluted your land and gave you some cheese in return?
Yeah.

Emeregildo always tells people how the cheese smelled strange to them, so they just left it in the forest.

Man-
In Italy you'd never let cheese go to waste...

you know...
Many of the Indigenous nationalities today are organizing against the oil companies.

They demand that they be consulted before drilling can proceed on their land, like the law says.
That's right.

A few years ago the Waorani won a legal case--
-- where they were able to prove that the company hadn't received consent to operate.

Yes, things have changed since the Texaco days.
Ropes ready!

We're about to dock. Enjoy your trip.
And don't forget--
--the Amazon is a magical place!

Oh, we'll remember!
yes, definitely.

Alright, take care Donald.
You too, see you around.
Bye bye.

Discoveries

Now you're really going to see what oil has done to the Amazon ...

AG-04

AGUARICO 04
PETRO AMAZONAS
Pozo Reinjector

In 1974, Texaco drilled the well on the platform where we parked the truck.
They operated the well for many years, until it wasn't productive anymore.
In 2000, Petroecuador turned the Aguarico-4 well into a reinjection well to send the production waters deep underground.
What you see here is one of many waste pits.
This one is about 3 meters deep, 15 meters long, and 25 meters wide.

This pit has been here for 37 years.
Horses and other animals have died here.
24 cows.
These pools are directly related to the problems you see in the area.
This pit was never covered over. Texaco says it is the legal responsibility of Petroecuador due to a remediation contract in the 1990s.
But Texaco built and operated it.

This is the territory of the Siona, Sekoya, and the Cofán. It killed off what their people used to eat -- it killed their animals, their fish, it totally changed their way of life.
It killed their Sumak Kawsay.

Sumak Kawsay?
It means good life. It's an idea here in Ecuador that is based on the cosmovision of the Kichwa people.

It has to do with living in harmony with nature and people.
Isn't it related to that whole idea of giving nature legal standing? I've heard talk about that.

Well, yes, it's part of our 2008 Constitution. It's the idea that nature isn't just a natural resource to be used by humans, but it is an entity that has rights.
It means you can't separate the environment from culture because they are deeply connected.

Unfortunately, this was business.

They didn't cover it over, they just dumped it here.
They saved a huge amount of money by doing it this way.

They lit pits like this on fire.
There were columns of smoke that went on forever.

The planes would fly through the columns of smoke--
In the early years, there were two planes: one belonged to Texaco, the other to CEPE.

-- the pilots said that up in the sky the columns grew together, joining into a dark mass.
Today it's illegal to burn pits like this.

But--
But how was it possible that companies were allowed to do this?

These practices were designed to pollute.
They knew what they were doing.

Texaco didn't use the same operating techniques that they used in their US operations during that time.

It's just--
--it just makes me so angry that this company came here, to this fantastic place--
--and just did what they wanted in order to make money!

Well, umm...
Without giving a damn about the forest.
Or the rivers!
Or the people who lived here!

How is it possible that the government let this happen?
Unfortunately, stories like this are not so uncommon...

In many countries, the government was also interested in building up the industries like oil. So it wasn't just that they looked the other way. Like Donald said, the Ecuadorian state was also part of the consortium.
Right?

But because Texaco had far more experience in the industry, they were the technical manager and so they set the terms for the design, construction, installation, and operation of the oil industry here until about 1990.

This pipe was installed when the pit was built.
It smells like gas.
Hrmpf
The idea was that when the rains came, this pipe would allow the water to drain off so that the pit doesn't overflow.
But it's not just water that leaves the pit.
How is it possible that it continues to drain here after all these years?

Imagine all the communities below whose water is being contaminated by pits like this.

yeah, sometimes when we visit communities at work, they tell us that they know the water is bad --
--or that it's contaminated.

I have always wondered how they knew, or how they could say that without tests --
snif

-- because sometimes the water seemed fine to me.
Maybe it just had extra sediment in it, so it was cloudy or something.
But when you look at something like this that has been draining for so long--

--and think where all of this contamination goes--
--it's just so blatant.

It's terrible to think that the water you are drinking could be making you sick.

Yes. As you can see, the pit is connected to the stream back there.

And that stream connects to the Aguarico River.

The river flows through many, many communities.

And after that it reaches the Peruvian border, where it joins with the Napo River.

And finally--
--the Amazon River.

The contamination that has been seeping out of these pits for decades now affects not just those of us who live here in Ecuador--
--it affects everyone who relies on this water downstream.

So, who wants to walk on the pit?
Really?

Give it a try!
You can see for yourselves what it's like to stand on top of an oil pit. You can even find out how deep it is.

I don't know... Do you think it's safe?
Well, I've done it many, many times.

I'll try!

Careful!

Go ahead and shift your weight a bit.

Use this stick to see how deep the pit is under the layers of leaves.

Okay, let's see.

Nothing yet...
Gosh, it's really deep.

There it is! I think I can feel the bottom now.

Can you guys take a picture?
Sure!

Just give me a second.
It just keeps going ...
It's actually 2.5 meters deep. That's even taller than me!

Watch out!

clic
clic
clic

clic
clic
clic

We've got you, don't you worry!
snift
It's ok, Elena.

I just... Wow. I felt myself falling into the pit and I just...

I'm glad you didn't fall in all the way!
Now you can really say that you've been on a toxic tour!

And I've got the pictures to prove it--
--I'm sorry, but they're hilarious.
Oh, yeah...

Haha
sniff
You're right.
Look at my face!

Can you send me those?
Sure.

You know, it's happened to me and others who live here many times.
You have fallen in?
Oh yeah.
Yet another reason to have those pits cleaned up.

And we should get you cleaned up too. I have an extra pair of boots in the car

Here I thought I'd be jumping from a canoe into the Laguna Grande in the Cuyabeno, not falling off an old log into an oil pit.
Hehehe

Let's sit for a minute, there's lots more to discover here.

Encounters

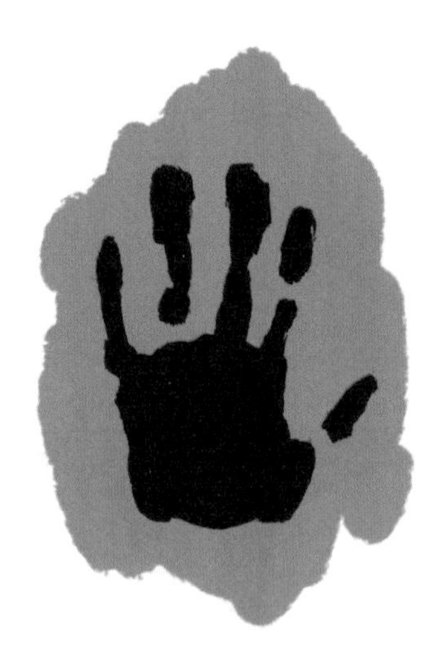

These pits are full of bad stuff, chemicals from drilling wastes that were just dumped here--

--heavy metals like in the formation waters...

There are also radioactive elements like iridium-190, uranium, thorium, strontium-90, radium-226 --
gasp

--and many other chemicals such as aluminum silicate, anionic polyacrylamide, caustic potash, sodium carbonate, barium sulfate--

-- salts, quicklime, sodium polychloride, beryllium, mica, and detergents.
...
...

These chemicals are harmful to human health.
Some of them irritate the eyes or lungs, others are known to be carcinogenic or cause problems for the nervous system.
...

And all that is on my boots?

We'll clean them off later. Good thing it's not on your legs!

And those are just the chemicals used in drilling. Crude oil itself also contains many components that are bad for human health.
Aromatic hydrocarbons, the kind that you can smell like benzene, toluene, and xylene.
There are also polycyclic aromatic hydrocarbons. These are so toxic that only two dozen nanograms per liter presents a risk of cancer.
And crude also contains gases and other heavy metals.
What's a na-no-gram?

It's an amount that is so tiny that it's impossible to see without special equipment.
Ohh.

So it's teeny tiny like this?
yes.

And maybe even smaller than that.
Whoa, really?
Are you guys drinking enough? The heat is killing me.

Good idea, Angela.
I have a jug in the truck where you can refill your bottles.

I remember reading once about how oil is formed from the biomass of the oceans, hundreds of millions of years ago.
It's wild to think that something that is "natural" can also be so poisonous.

Isn't it fascinating how what we use to run our cars or travel across the world all started as tiny marine plants and animals ages ago?

Well, and just think how long it took to form and how quickly we are using it up.
Right.

Exactly.
Right now we are sitting over one of those pockets of crude, which is buried about 1,800-2,000 meters below the surface.

When they drilled the new wells, they had to figure out how productive they were.
So what did they do?
They would allow the well to drain into the pits next to the platform for 24, sometimes 48 hours.
This would tell them how productive a well was going to be and allow them to estimate how many barrels per day it would produce.

Then, as operations went on, they'd dump anything in there.

Trash.
Drilling muds.
Other things they discarded from the platform.

Of course Elena isn't the only one who has fallen into a pit. Like I told you before, sometimes people lost their horses, cows, and dogs in here.

And we find birds that have died, wings black with oil.

And imagine what happened to those animals ...

But have things changed since the earlier years under the consortium?
Yes, now it's much better.

Why?
Well, they don't dump oil on the roads, which is very important.
They also don't burn the oil in the pits, like they did before.

In the past, they would burn the gas not in gas flares--
--but through a lower burner directly over the pit itself.

The water in the pits contained crude particulates that would burn along with the gas.
Day and night.

Night and day.

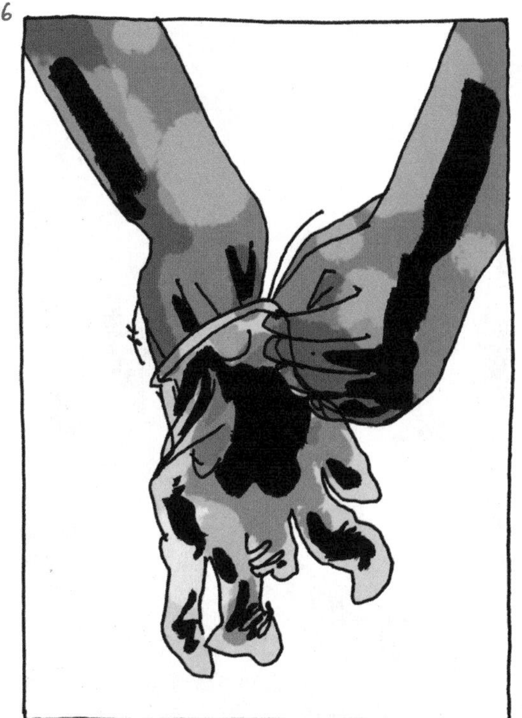

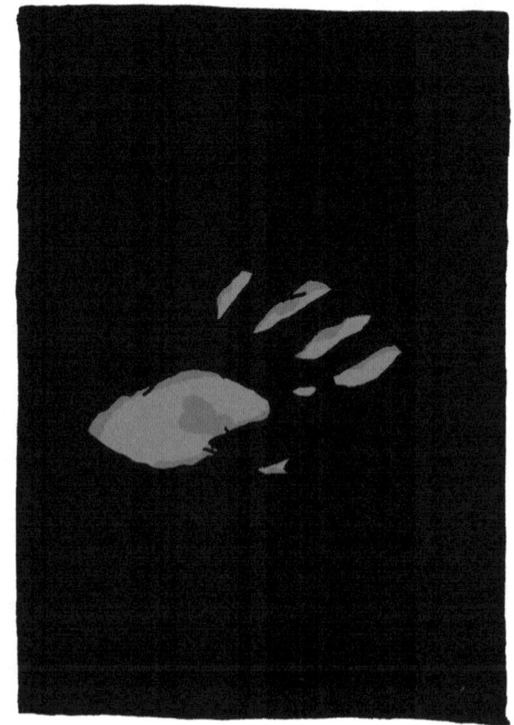

This is the price that the Amazon has paid for the oil that was extracted here.

Here, you guys can touch and smell it for yourselves.

This--
--what we are doing here today--

--this is uncovering the lie told by Texaco and so many others that oil isn't poisonous.
Or that the contamination that was here in the Amazon has been cleaned up.

Now I am going to take you to meet someone who has been deeply affected by oil.

So you can see what these waste pits, spills, and flares have done to our lives.

Stories

Buen día, compañera.

This is my friend, Yolanda. She has offered to tell you a bit about her life living alongside the oil operations.

A los tiempos! Cómo has estado?
Bien, bien, gracias.
Thanks for having us!

Come, please, we can sit over here.

Would you like some lemonade?
My son picked them this morning.

Thanks for coming today to listen to my story.

I came to the Amazon when I was 22. I was offered a job as a school teacher, so I left my family in the Sierra.
I had never seen oil before, but I had heard about the success of "black gold" in the Oriente.

When I arrived, everything was covered in oil. It stained our shoes, and our clothes. We would walk on the roads that had been covered in oil.
We were surrounded by all these bad smells.

Out in the sun, your body would burn, and you'd feel overwhelmed by the heat and the fumes.

Here you go, love.
Thanks.

Thanks, yola.
Papá, can I go play?
Sure.

First my post was on the Napo River, downstream from Coca, Sacha, and San Carlos, all places where oil extraction was starting.

The contaminated waters from upstream operations floated by us, and soon I started to feel sick.

Since there weren't any water wells yet, we'd drink water from the river.
We'd cook with water from the river.
We'd wash with the water directly from the river.

And you'd see small particles, like stains of black floating in the water, which you knew was surely oil.

And so then, after 6 months of working there, I got sick.
The same sickness I have today.

As you can see, my body is covered with these painful sores.

Oh, that must be awful.

Terrible.
Yes, everyday is like this.

So I went to the director of my school and asked to be moved to a town that was closer to a health center, so that I could get help .
That's when they told me to move here, to 12 de Febrero.

But what I didn't know was that by moving closer to roads, electricity, and health centers in these urbanizing areas of the Amazon--
--this meant that I was also moving closer to oil operations.

By the time I arrived here in 12 de Febrero, where I have been living ever since, there were already over 20 wells in the community.
I have to receive treatment constantly. So, I started traveling farther away to El Eden, and then to Quito, then to Guayaquil, looking for medication, but nobody knew what was wrong.

I am so tired of taking medication, just trying to feel a bit better.

Wow, that's a long trip just to go see a doctor.
Yes, It's about 16 hours by bus to get to Guayaquil from here.

Plus the cost of going and staying overnight. It's just miserable, especially when you don't feel well.
I would get sick from all the curves of the road and the heat alone.

So, since I started getting sick, up to today I've never found a cure.
Treatment, yes. But it continues to affect me.

It never goes away.
It has affected my adrenal glands, my stomach, as well as my lungs.

But what's the diagnosis?

Well, in the end, they don't know.

...
They don't know?

No, the doctors aren't able to say why I have these problems.

But I know that it must be from drinking contaminated water and breathing in contaminated air.
Day in and day out.

Unfortunately, Yolanda is one of many people here who have suffered like this. And many aren't here to tell their stories today.

It's very brave of you to share your story with us.
...

In the end--
--what I wish the most is to have my skin strong again.

My skin is like the skin of a tomato – but I think that even tomato skin is stronger.

Any kind of bump, or when I run into something, it breaks open.

And the worst is, when I get these lesions they ooze and hurt.
It must be awful to suffer like that for so long.

What the Texaco Company did when they operated here is heartbreaking--
--the formation waters--

--the spills they caused--
--no cleanup--
--the lack of treatment.

They just used the environment as though it didn't belong to anyone. People came to the Amazon to finally have land to farm, to get out of poverty.
And they thought that this was normal for the oil industry.

You mean that you didn't realize something was wrong when the companies dumped oil and lit the pits on fire?
We didn't know.
Nobody told us that it could be harmful to live next door to it.
And besides: where else were we supposed to get water?
Or farm our animals and grow our crops?
There was no alternative.

Then afterwards, when people started getting sick, when people started suffering from strange diseases, then we realized.
In this area, no one insists, no one inquires, no one sees. There's no newspaper, no press. Nothing.
It's just criminal what's been happening to people like you.
The way they operated was completely inhumane and unethical.

They only thought about how much money they were making.
They only thought of profit.

And it has to be said that some of the authorities have been complicit.
Complicit?

Mmh ...
Today we are seeing the consequences.

People who are young -- like Donald, like you, even younger, are dying of strange diseases.

...

you know
...

You know, when the women would go to the river to bathe, rashes and skin spots would coat the arms, bellies, and backs of their children, of their babies.
Many people have gotten sick after bathing in the river following a spill of formation waters or crude oil.
Or one woman, she had a miscarriage after washing clothes in the river one day after there had been a spill of formation waters upstream.
Others have developed uterine cancer.

Over there--
Their daughter died from cancer, she was 3 years old.
...
Over here, Don Suárez died, where the spills are.
3 spills.
Over here, Don Larrea died, also from cancer.
This neighbor had two daughters who died from unknown diseases--
--probably cancer, they didn't even know what from.
My good friend, Señora Bastidas is gone as well.

Señor Romero, a man my husband's age, died from cancer.
He left for Quito and came back in a box.

My god.
Of the cases I have seen, more than 15 people have died from cancer in 12 de Febrero.

If we were to go up to well 28, there are various other cases, where people have fallen in the pits--
--trying to save animals that have fallen in.

And there are other cases where people won't even speak about what happened.
People are desperate.

You see those flares over there?

Sometimes we get headaches so bad that we can't work.
Other times I see that my son's eyes are red and itchy.

Or our throats get scratchy and our chests are too tight to breathe.

The flares leave ashy traces all over our water tanks and the leaves of our plants.

They used to light the waste pits on fire--
--and the fire would make these terrible columns of smoke.

Black but thick, like when you're making marmalade.
And in each part of these columns, you'd see this big, thick cloud.
That's how it was.

It would start like that and then within an hour and a half or so, then it would rain.
And with the rain, all of this smoke rained down.
Stained all the plants, the clothes on the line too if they were outside.

Sometimes we weren't at home and when we got back, all of the laundry would be stained black. We wouldn't have anything to wear.
Everything was bathed in this toxic rain.

It would damage the roofs of the houses and we wouldn't have any water.
...

And the water tanks that we had started to build would be covered too.

Were you worried about staying here?

Well, yes, dear. Of course.

We were worried too when the animals started getting sick.

Also when the dog started losing its fur after going through the river.
And when the pigs died after a spill on my father's farm.

But where else were we supposed to go? Contaminated land is worth very little.
And we have made our lives here.

We want to see this place cleaned up as it should be.

And obvi...
Hola!

Buenos días! Hola Donald.
Cómo va? Quieres almorzar?

Gracias mamá.

That's my son. He works as a security guard for the station over the hill.

He works for the oil company?
Well,
In a way, yes. It's hard to find jobs around here.

Lots of people here have worked for the oil companies, or other oil services, at one point.
You gotta find a way to make ends meet.
Or maybe you open up a restaurant ...
And who are most of the customers?

The oil workers.
Hmm...

I guess I would have thought that people around here wouldn't want to work in oil.
Right?

You know--
--it's not that people here are necessarily opposed to oil extraction.

But...
But after all the oil companies have done?
Well, yes, there are people who are opposed to oil development, of course.

But what many people are ultimately bothered by is the attitude of some companies, who act like they don't care about those of us who live here.

The companies come in and say they're going to operate with state of the art technology.
And, well--
--I wish they would.

Oil production is never going to be clean, but at least they need to do their best so that honest people can live a dignified life here.

you know, clean up the messes that were made decades ago--
--and clean up the messes that they are making now.

But don't you wish that they would end oil production in the Amazon?
Go back to how life was before?

Well, of course I wish we could just be done with oil.
We can't go back to how things were before.

But we can work on making things better now.

Clean up what needs to be cleaned up.

Donald has been doing a lot of work trying to hold companies, including the ones run by the Ecuadorian state, accountable.

Yola, that reminds me --
--I brought these papers for you to sign.

This one is for the legal efforts we are involved in, trying to get them to clean up a spill on a neighbor's farm.

People like Donald make this work possible.
We're all in it together.

Well, Yola, I think we have to get going.
Thanks for spending the afternoon with us.

Anytime, Donald.

Thanks for listening.
Thank you for sharing.

Yes, thanks very much, Yolanda.
And thanks for the lemonade.

I'll be in touch next week.

Dreams

You guys are probably starving, right?

Luckily--

--I know the best place to get maitos, it's a local favorite.

Aaand... here we are.

Buenas!

I just realized how hungry I am.
Same!
Totally.

Makes you think, right?
About where all these products come from.

Yeah, I was just thinking about all the different ways my life is dependent on oil...

Like to be able to take this job here, I had to fly from Italy.
And then every day we drive the truck around town and use all these products that are made from plastic.

I never really thought about it before.
Like where does the oil come from that makes all this possible?

Yes.
For me it's incredible to think about all the lives that are affected in the process of extracting crude to making something like this cup.

Are you glad you came on the tour today?
Glad?

Well, that wouldn't be the first word that comes to mind.

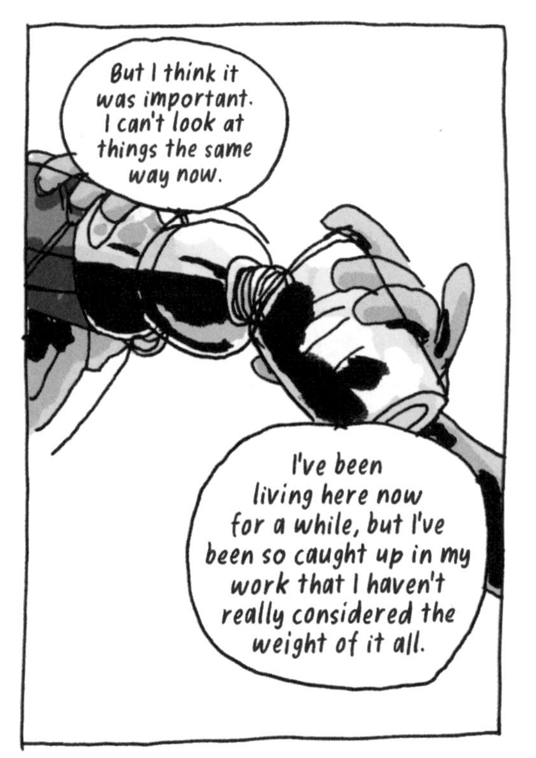
But I think it was important. I can't look at things the same way now.
I've been living here now for a while, but I've been so caught up in my work that I haven't really considered the weight of it all.

Do you guys want some more?
Please.
I just keep thinking of my hometown--

If this were to happen there -- would I stay?
I don't know.

I guess when you're surrounded by oil wells, what does it mean to have a "clean" environment?

I was thinking about how, for many of the people in the communities we work with--
--it's hard to make ends meet each month.
Coming up with the money to move would be near impossible.

On the other hand, how could you just stay, knowing you were breathing and drinking all those toxic things?
Living next to all those chemicals?

This is the difficult situation that so many of us find ourselves in.
We wonder about our health, or our children's health, every day.

But this is our home.

For many people here, we don't want to leave.
We love this place, and we're here to fight for it.

Most of all, we want to see it cleaned up.

This is the problem with thinking about contamination as though one can just move away from it.
The same thing happens in California where I live. We are very close to the refinery.
Sometimes people see us protesting and they say:
"Why don't you just move somewhere else in the city?"
But we can't "just move." It's not the point.

How could you turn over your house or land which you know is contaminated to another family for them to live on and suffer the same thing?

I guess it's a problem of thinking that contamination can be contained--
--that you can just leave it behind, or cover it up, and the problems will go away.

Looking at the gooseneck pipe really got me thinking about all the ways that the contamination of this pit was seeping, drop by drop, into the stream below.

And how, maybe--
--when someone comes to fish or swim downstream, they don't know what they are coming in contact with.

It's never just about contamination in one spot...

When you think about how contaminated water travels, it becomes so hard to contain the contami--

Alé!

Here-
This should help with your spill.

Just think:
What we saw today was just a small sliver of the total operations here.

Sometimes I take people to see pineapple that is growing for commercial sale. And when you dig down underneath it, crude oil comes up.
Just think when those pineapples arrive at the markets--

--not just in Ecuador but elsewhere, too--
--people have no idea what they might be eating.

People come here to go on a toxic tour and see how oil has transformed this part of the Amazon.
But it's not only the people who live here who are dependent on oil.

This oil makes our lives as well as so many other lives around the world possible.
The difference is--

--here in Lago Agrio and the surrounding areas, we have lived the cost of extracting that oil in our bodies, in our soils, and rivers.

Oh, here comes the food.
Have you guys ever had maitos before?
No.

Pati, could you explain?
Well--

-- I hope you all like fish and yuca.
It's been steamed in plaintain leaves, so it's really juicy.

Enjoy!

Wow, it smells amazing.

...

What kind of hopes do you have for Lago Agrio, Donald?

The city is a different place than what it was before.
And the people have changed too.

This was long before you were born, my love.
Now you can see all the progress that has been made.

The new Millenium Park, for instance.
People here are aware now of what oil does to the environment.

But what will happen when the oil is used up?

Well, I think we're already moving into a time of post-oil. Oil drilling has been moving south to other cities -- like Coca, for instance -- in these past few years.

This is the thing about oil --the profit is so short lived.
It is clear that we need to have other models for how we can live and grow--

--without depending on a resource that causes so much harm for such fleeting benefit.

YES!
But just because the city is changing--

--like there are people working to use low-cost technologies like mushrooms to remediate contaminated soils--
--or working to create health networks--

--it doesn't mean that oil is gone.
Oil is still present in many ways--
--and certainly the legacy of contamination remains here.

That is something that we will have to deal with every day of our lives.
Not just the oil extraction that is going on today--

--or the spill that ruined Don Gonzalo's water yesterday.
The remnants of old contamination still haven't been cleaned up.

I just want people to know what happened here and help us get justice.
To help us get this place cleaned up--
--and to learn from our stuggle, so that it doesn't happen anywhere else.

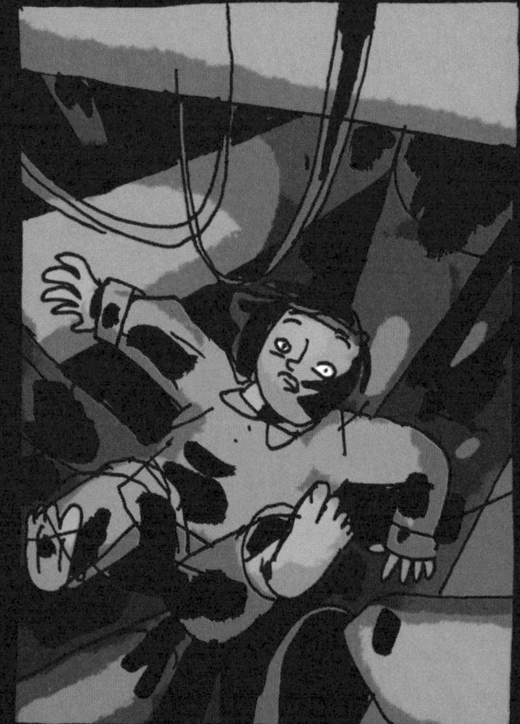

Dong
Dong

Dong
Dong

Ecco il suo caffè.

Perfetto, grazie.

Scusi?!

Cough
Cough

Bzzz
bzzz

Hola, Mamá.
pop

Yes.
Yes, it was good.
Yes, I'm finally going to the Cuyabeno today.

Yes...
Yes, I'll call when I arrive.

Good morning, Papá.
Good morning.

Do you have another tour today?
Mhhm, yes.
Where are they from? Americans again?
Nope
Hm
From Italy?

This time it's a German artist and an old friend.
You were very little the last time you met her.

Can I come along?
And can I bring my cousin too?
Sure.
We'll pick her up on the way.

Papá?

Hmm?
Maybe on Saturday we can go to the river? Go for a swim?

Yay!
Yes.
Good plan, my dear.

Amelia Fiske & Jonas Fischer, 2023

"I do not charge for toxic tours.
I do it for education.
I do it to raise awareness of the
serious environmental problem that
we have on our planet, which has
been severely affected by industries,
including oil, mining, and coal.
Today this is clearly seen in the
contempt that nature has towards
humankind through the effects
of climate change."

Donald Moncayo
7 March 2023

Get Involved

Looking to get involved or learn more about oil contamination in Ecuador? The **Unión de Afectados y Afectadas por las Operaciones Petroleras de Texaco** (UDAPT; Union of People Affected by Texaco Oil Operations) is a nonprofit organization formed by Indigenous and settler groups to lead the community response to the *Aguinda v. Texaco* lawsuit. As such, UDAPT represents the voices of more than 30,000 people who have been affected by Texaco's operations across an area of 450,000 acres in the northeastern Ecuadorian Amazon. All decisions taken by UDAPT pass through the review and approval of their base communities.

One of UDAPT's principal objectives is to fight for reparations and remediation of the environment affected by contamination from Texaco and other companies that have operated in the area. UDAPT has conducted environmental monitoring and scientific surveys of the health effects of contamination from oil activities, and it partners with many other local organizations. UDAPT also maintains an active social media presence, including publishing reports on the *Aguinda* process and supporting ongoing campaigns such as those to end gas flaring in Sucumbíos, Orellana, Pastaza, and Napo provinces.

Go on a toxic tour! UDAPT is also responsible for organizing the toxic tours like the ones that inspired this book. There is no charge for the tour itself, only for the price of transportation to visit the contaminated sites. Toxic tours can be tailored to the specific interests of the participants. If you would like to plan a tour, please contact UDAPT at the address below.

UDAPT
Av. Venezuela 902 y Progreso, Edificio ACOPSAS
Lago Agrio, Ecuador
Email: udapt1993@gmail.com
http://texacotoxico.net/en/

Organizations Working in the Region on Environmental Health Issues

Acción Ecológica is a leading environmental organization in Ecuador that has been active in the region since the 1980s. It has coordinated campaigns and research studies that make visible the effects of oil operations on life in the Amazon. https://www.accionecologica.org/

Amazon Frontlines is an international team living in the Amazon rainforest committed to the fight for Indigenous autonomy and rainforest protection. https://amazonfrontlines.org/

Amazon Watch is a nonprofit organization dedicated to protecting the rainforest and advancing the rights of Indigenous peoples in the Amazon basin. https://amazonwatch.org/

Ceibo Alliance is an Indigenous-led organization, composed of members of the Siona, Siekopai, A'i Cofán, and Waorani nations, focused on protecting Indigenous land, life, and cultural survival in the upper Amazon. https://amazonfrontlines.org/videos-categorias/ceibo-alliance/

Clínica Ambiental brings together local communities and a range of professionals committed to socio-environmental repair and focuses on increasing the role of popular and community-led scientific research. https://www.clinicambiental.org/

Frente de Defensa de la Amazonía was established in 1994 to represent the interests of the affected Indigenous and settler communities in the *Aguinda v. Texaco* lawsuit. It works to defend local communities from extractive harm resulting from oil, mining, and agriculture.

Teaching Exercises

These exercises are intended to spark discussion and reflection around both the use of graphic techniques and the ethnographic themes of this book, including toxicity, oil development, and environmental justice. In some cases, additional reading or research may be needed for the exercises to be successful. Adapt as best suited for your needs and interests.

1 When incorporating visual exercises into the classroom, it's often helpful to begin with some warm-ups. There are many drawing warm-up exercises; we have included a couple here:

Pick partners and sit opposite one another. You each will need something to draw with and a piece of paper. Set a timer for 30 seconds. Looking directly at your partner, begin to draw them without looking at the paper. When the timer goes off, stop drawing and share your portraits with each other. The point is not to create a "realistic" portrait, but rather to pay close attention to the person you are drawing and to have fun. This can be done as a quick warm-up, swapping partners after the first round, and as a way for students to get to know one another.

As a variation on the former, pick a partner and sit opposite one another. Set a timer for 30 seconds. Looking straight at your partner, begin to draw them without looking at the paper. This time do not lift your pen or pencil from the paper; the entire exercise should be done with one continuous line. When the timer goes off, stop drawing and share your portraits with each other.

For a longer drawing exercise: Sit with your eyes closed. The facilitator will hand each participant a different object for them to hold. Set a timer for five minutes. Observe the object with your hands, focusing on what you can learn about it through the sense of touch. When the timer goes off, the facilitator collects all objects and instructs the participants to open their eyes. Each person then draws their object from memory. When finished, the facilitator places all the objects on the table for participants to see. Each participant displays their image for the group, and another participant selects the object that inspired it from the collection on the table. When all objects and drawings have been matched, participants then draw the object anew, this time by sight. To conclude, the group can discuss what can be learned by attending to different senses in drawing exercises.

2 What choices were made in the selection of the book's cover? Think about what aspects of the story you would choose to emphasize and design a new cover. Create a jacket for the book using a piece paper that is slightly larger than the book itself. Fold the edges over so that the book jacket completely covers the book. On the back cover, write your own summary of the graphic novel and review its strengths and weaknesses.
3 Think of a place you know well, such as a place you grew up or one where you have spent a lot of time. If you were to give people who were not from that place a tour, what would you want them to know? Where would you take them? What should they see, smell, hear, touch, or taste firsthand to understand what you would like to convey about the place? Is there someone you would want them to meet in order to tell them about a particular aspect of the place? Draw a map of your tour.
4 Graphic novels use a number of visual tools and techniques to tell a story, which makes the genre distinct from illustration. Working in groups, research some of the technical components of a graphic novel (panel, frame, gutter, written words or speech bubbles, sound effects, motion lines, color, foreground/midground/background, change in perspective, symbolism, foreshadowing, etc.). Then analyze how these technical aspects are used to tell the story of *Toxic*. What choices were made in the visual execution of the book, and how do they work together to tell a particular kind of story and to create meaning? What is shown and what is not shown in relation to toxicity, oil development, or environmental justice?
5 Pick a chapter from the book. Diagram the chapter and convert it into written notes. Which elements of the story are more challenging to "convert" from visuals into words? Which elements are easier?
6 What can be conveyed about toxicity through graphic art that cannot be conveyed through prose or other scientific forms of writing? Consider how you might express some of the concepts from the book in a different format, such as in poetry, song, dance, or theater? What do you think would be lost, and what would be gained in the process of choosing another modality?

7 Choose one character and draft an additional chapter for the end of the book about that character. For example, where might Angela, Elena, or Gianluca go next? How do they incorporate their experiences from the tour into their lives? Or imagine what Donald, Leo, or Yolanda do following the tour. Draw it in the form of a storybook. Exchange with a classmate and explain how and why your chapter changes the story.
8 Select a book chapter, academic article, or news story that you have read recently and found interesting. Take notes as you reread it, paying attention to what the author is trying to impart and the most important images that come to mind. Then create a storyboard to visually convey the chapter or article. Many chapters or articles may be too long for this exercise; in that case, pick one specific section to focus on for your storyboard.
9 While dominant narratives privilege the perspectives of individuals or groups in power, counter narratives are designed to give voice to the perspectives of those who have been marginalized, creating a space to resist forms of domination and naturalized assumptions about how the world is organized. Counter narratives often draw on individual and community experiences to challenge mainstream, hegemonic assumptions or descriptions of how things came to be. To what extent does Donald's toxic tour function as a counter narrative? Which perspectives are brought to the fore, and which perspectives would you like to know more about? If you could go on a tour, who else would you want to speak with? What else would you want to know?
10 While toxicants may be a universal problem, their distribution and burden are never borne equally. Across the world, Indigenous communities have long been living alongside sites of contamination and extraction, and communities of color have historically and repeatedly borne undue burdens of toxic waste and environmental racism. Distributions of poor health and industrial waste traverse pre-existing contours of position and power, including race, class, gender, and political economy. Discuss how this case converges or diverges with the environmental justice movements in different places. What might various environmental justice struggles around the world have in common? Where do they diverge? To what extent is it productive to think about environmental justice matters like the one recounted in *Toxic* as a "local" or "global" question?

Further Reading

Want to read further on matters of oil, extraction, contamination, exposure, toxic tours, environmental justice, Ecuador, or other topics that are mentioned in this book? Here are a few places to start:

Aguinda v. Texaco Lawsuit and Environmental Law

Acosta, Alberto. 2011. "Sentencia a la Chevron-Texaco, un triunfo de la humanidad." Observatorio de Derechos Colectivos del Ecuador. https://odjec.org.

Barrett, Paul M. 2014. *Law of the Jungle: The $19 Billion Legal Battle over Oil in the Rain Forest and the Lawyer Who'd Stop at Nothing to Win*. New York: Crown.

Berlinger, Joe. 2009. *Crude: The Real Price of Oil*. DVD. New York: First Run Features.

Fajardo Mendoza, Pablo, Julio Prieto Méndez, and Juan Pablo Sáenz. 2011. *Summary of Part One of Plaintiffs' Alegato Final (Final Argument) in Environmental Disaster Litigation Against Chevron*. Published online by the Amazon Defense Coalition on January 24, 2011. https://chevroninecuador.org/news-and-multimedia/2011/0124-summary-of-final-argument-part-1

Kimerling, Judith. 1991. *Amazon Crude*. New York: Natural Resources Defense Council.

Kimerling, Judith. 1996. *El derecho del tambor*. Quito: Abya-Yala Ediciones.

Kimerling, Judith. 2006a. "Indigenous Peoples and the Oil Frontier in Amazonia: The Case of Ecuador, ChevronTexaco, and Aguinda v. Texaco." *New York University Journal of International Law and Politics* 38: 413–664. https://nyujilp.org/wp-content/uploads/2013/02/38.3-Kimerling.pdf.

Kimerling, Judith. 2006b. "Transnational Operations, Bi-National Injustice: ChevronTexaco and Indigenous Huaorani and Kichwa in the Amazon Rainforest in Ecuador." *American Indian Law Review* 31: 445. https://doi.org/10.2307/20070795.

Kimerling, Judith. 2013. "Lessons from the Chevron Ecuador Litigation: The Proposed Intervenors' Perspective." *Stanford Journal of Complex Litigation* (SJCL) 1, no. 2: 241. https://law.stanford.edu/wp-content/uploads/2018/05/kimerling.pdf.

Kohn, Joseph, Myles Malman, Martin D'Urso, Diana Liberto, Cristobal Bonifaz, John Bonifaz, Steven Donziger, and Amy Damen. 1993. *Aguinda et. al. v. Texaco Inc.* 1–37. United States District Court for the Southern District of New York.

Oil, Extraction, and Related Conversations in Ecuador

Acosta, Alberto. 2009a. *Derechos de la naturaleza: El futuro es ahora*. Quito: Abya Yala.
Acosta, Alberto. 2009b. *El buen vivir*. Quito: Abya Yala.
Bustamante, Teodoro, ed. 2007. *Detrás de la cortina de humo: Dinámicas sociales y petróleo en el Ecuador*. Quito: FLACSO–Sede Ecuador.
Cepek, Michael. 2018. *Life in Oil: Cofán Survival in the Petroleum Fields of Amazonia*. Austin: University of Texas Press.
Dematteis, Lou, and Kayana Szymczak. 2008. *Crude Reflections/Cruda realidad: Oil, Ruin and Resistance in the Amazon Rainforest*. San Francisco: City Lights.
Fiske, Amelia. 2023. *Reckoning with Harm: The Toxic Relations of Oil in Amazonia*. Austin: University of Texas Press.
Fontaine, Guillaume. 2007. *El precio del petroleo*. Quito: Editorial Abya Yala.
Gudynas, Eduardo. 2009b. *El mandato ecológico: Derechos de la naturaleza y políticas ambientales en la nueva constitución*. Quito: Abya Yala.
Gudynas, Eduardo. 2011. "Buen Vivir: Today's Tomorrow." *Development* 54 (4): 441–447. https://doi.org/10.1057/dev.2011.86.
Larrea, Carlos, and Lavinia Warnars. 2009. "Ecuador's Yasuni-ITT Initiative: Avoiding Emissions by Keeping Petroleum Underground." *Energy for Sustainable Development* 13 (3): 219–223. https://doi.org/10.1016/j.esd.2009.08.003.
Lu, Flora, Gabriela Valdivia, and Néstor L. Silva. 2017. *Oil, Revolution, and Indigenous Citizenship in Ecuadorian Amazonia*. New York: Palgrave Macmillan.
Maldonado, Adolfo, and Alberto Narváez. 2003. *Ecuador ni es, ni será ya país amazónico: Inventario de impactos petroleros*. Quito: Acción Ecológica.
Riofrancos, Thea. 2020. *Resource Radicals: From Petro-Nationalism to Post-Extractivism in Ecuador*. Durham: Duke University Press.
Sawyer, Suzana. 2004. *Crude Chronicles: Indigenous Politics, Multinational Oil, and Neoliberalism in Ecuador*. Durham: Duke University Press.
Sawyer, Suzana. 2022. *The Small Matter of Suing Chevron*. Durham: Duke University Press.
Viteri Toro, Jorge. 2008. *Petroleo, lanzas y sangre*. Quito: Ministerio de Minas y Petroleos.

Exposure Scholarship

Alaimo, Stacy. 2016. *Exposed: Environmental Politics and Pleasures in Posthuman Times*. Minneapolis: University of Minnesota Press.
Bohme, Susanna Rankin. 2014. *Toxic Injustice: A Transnational History of Exposure and Struggle*. Berkeley: University of California Press.
Brown, Phil. 2007. *Toxic Exposures: Contested Illnesses and the Environmental Health Movement*. New York: Columbia University Press.

Davis, Devra. 2003. *When Smoke Ran Like Water: Tales of Environmental Deception and the Battle against Pollution*. New York: Basic Books.
Fiske, Amelia. 2018. "Dirty Hands: The Toxic Politics of Denunciation." *Social Studies of Science* 48 (3): 389–413. https://doi.org/10.1177/0306312718781505.
Fiske, Amelia. 2020b. "Naked in the Face of Contamination. Thinking Models and Metaphors of Toxicity Together." *Catalyst: Feminism, Theory, Technoscience* 6(1): 1–30. https://doi.org/10.28968/cftt.v6i1.32093.
Lamoreaux, Janelle. 2016. "What if the Environment Is a Person? Lineages of Epigenetic Science in a Toxic China." *Cultural Anthropology* 31 (2): 188–214. https://doi.org/10.14506/ca31.2.03.
Langston, Nancy. 2010. *Toxic Bodies: Hormone Disruptors and the Legacy of DES*. New Haven: Yale University Press.
Lerner, Steve. 2010. *Sacrifice Zones: The Front Lines of Toxic Chemical Exposure in the United States*. Cambridge: MIT Press.
Liboiron, Max. 2021. *Pollution Is Colonialism*. Durham: Duke University Press.
Murphy, Michelle. 2017. "Alterlife and Decolonial Chemical Relations." *Cultural Anthropology* 32 (4): 494–503. https://doi.org/10.14506/ca32.4.02.
Nading, Alex M. 2020. "Living in a Toxic World." *Annual Review of Anthropology* 49 (1): 209–224. https://doi.org/10.1146/annurev-anthro-010220-074557.
Nash, Linda. 2007. *Inescapable Ecologies: A History of Environment, Disease, and Knowledge.* Berkeley: University of California Press.
Roberts, Elizabeth. 2017. "What Gets Inside: Violent Entanglements and Toxic Boundaries in Mexico City." *Cultural Anthropology* 32 (4): 592–619. https://doi.org/10.14506/ca32.4.07.
Shapiro, Nicholas. 2015. "Attuning to the Chemosphere: Domestic Formaldehyde, Bodily Reasoning, and the Chemical Sublime." *Cultural Anthropology* 30 (3): 368–393. https://doi.org/10.14506/ca30.3.02.
Simmons, Kristen. 2017. "Settler Atmospherics." *Member Voices, Fieldsights*, November 20, 2017. https://culanth.org/fieldsights/1221-settler-atmospherics.
Tousignant, Noémi. 2018. *Edges of Exposure: Toxicology and the Problem of Capacity in Postcolonial Senegal.* Durham: Duke University Press.
Wylie, Sara Ann. 2018. *Fractivism: Corporate Bodies and Chemical Bonds*. Durham: Duke University Press.

Environmental Justice

Brulle, Robert, and David Pellow. 2006. "Environmental Justice: Human Health and Environmental Inequalities." *Annual Review of Public Health* 27 (1): 103–124. https://doi.org/10.1146/annurev.publhealth.27.021405.102124.
Bullard, Robert D. 2001. "Environmental Justice in the 21st Century: Race Still Matters." *Phylon* 49 (3–4): 151–171. https://doi.org/10.2307/3132626.
Checker, Melissa. 2005. *Polluted Promises: Environmental Racism and the Search for Justice in a Southern Town*. New York: NYU Press.
Fiske, Amelia. 2020a. "The Auger: A Tool of Environmental Justice in Ecuadorian Toxic Tours." In *Toxic Truths: Environmental Justice and Citizen Science in a Post-Truth Age*, edited by Thom Davies and Alice Mah, 124–139. Manchester: Manchester University Press.

Hoover, Elizabeth. 2017. *The River Is in Us: Fighting Toxics in a Mohawk Community*. Minneapolis: University of Minnesota Press.
McGregor, Deborah. 2018. "Mino-Mnaamodzawin: Achieving Indigenous Environmental Justice in Canada." *Environment and Society* 9 (1): 7–24. https://doi.org/10.3167/ares.2018.090102.
Ott, Riki. 2008. *Not One Drop: Betrayal and Courage in the Wake of the Exxon Valdez Oil Spill*. White River Junction: Chelsea Green Publishing.
Pellow, David. 2007. *Resisting Global Toxics: Transnational Movements for Environmental Justice*. Cambridge: MIT Press.
Pezzullo, Phaedra Carmen. 2009. *Toxic Tourism: Rhetorics of Pollution, Travel, and Environmental Justice*. Tuscaloosa: University of Alabama Press.
Robins, Nicholas, and Barbara Fraser, eds. 2020. *Landscapes of Inequity: Environmental Justice in the Andes-Amazon Region*. Lincoln: University of Nebraska Press.

Extraction

Cielo, Cristina, and Lisset Coba. 2018. "Extractivism, Gender, and Disease: An Intersectional Approach to Inequalities." *Ethics & International Affairs* 32 (2): 169–178. https://doi.org/10.1017/S0892679418000291.
Cielo, Cristina, Lisset Coba, and Ivette Vallejo. 2016. "Women, Nature, and Development in Sites of Ecuador's Petroleum Circuit: Ecuador's Petroleum Circuit." *Economic Anthropology* 3 (1): 119–132. https://doi.org/10.1002/sea2.12049.
Davidov, Veronica. 2013. "Mining versus Oil Extraction: Divergent and Differentiated Environmental Subjectivities in 'Post-Neoliberal' Ecuador." *Journal of Latin American and Caribbean Anthropology* 18 (3): 485–504. https://doi.org/10.1111/jlca.12043.
Fiske, Amelia. 2017a. "Bounded Impacts, Boundless Promise: Environmental Impact Assessments of Oil Production in the Ecuadorian Amazon." In *ExtrACTION: Impacts, Engagements and Alternative Futures*, edited by Kirk Jalbert, Anna Willow, David Casagrande, and Stephanie Paladino, 63–76. London: Routledge.
Fiske, Amelia. 2017b. "Natural Resources by Numbers." *Environment and Society* 8 (1): 125–143. https://doi.org/10.3167/ares.2017.080106.
Gómez-Barris, Macarena. 2017. *The Extractive Zone: Social Ecologies and Decolonial Perspectives*. Durham: Duke University Press.
Gudynas, Eduardo. 2009a. "Diez tesis urgentes sobre el nuevo extractivismo: Contextos y demandas bajo el progresismo sudamericano actual." In *Extractivismo, política y sociedad*, edited by Jürgen Schuldt, Alberto Acosta, Alberto Barandiarán, Anthony Bebbington, Mauricio Folchi, CEDLA – Bolivia, Alejandra Alayza, and Eduardo Gudynas, 187–225. Quito: Centro Andino de Acción Popular y Centro Latino Americano de Ecología Social.
Li, Fabiana. 2015. *Unearthing Conflict: Corporate Mining, Activism, and Expertise in Peru*. Durham: Duke University Press.
Lyall, Angus, and Gabriela Valdivia. 2019. "The Speculative Petro-State: Volatile Oil Prices and Resource Populism in Ecuador." *Annals of the American Association of Geographers* 109 (2): 349–360. https://doi.org/10.1080/24694452.2018.1531690.

Martínez Novo, Carmen. 2021. *Undoing Multiculturalism: Resource Extraction and Indigenous Rights in Ecuador.* Pittsburgh: University of Pittsburgh Press.
Riofrancos, Thea. 2017. "Extractivismo Unearthed: A Genealogy of a Radical Discourse." *Cultural Studies* 31 (2–3): 277–306. https://doi.org/10.1080/09502386.2017.1303429.
Roca-Servat, Denisse, and Jenni Perdomo-Sánchez (compilers). 2020. *La lucha por los comunes y las alternativas al desarrollo frente al extractivismo.* Buenos Aires: CLACSO.

Health Effects of Oil in Ecuador

Beristain, Carlos Martín, Darío Páez Rovira, and Itziar Fernández. 2009. *Las palabras de la selva: Estudio psicosocial del impacto de las explotaciones petroleras de Texaco en las comunidades amazónicas de Ecuador*. Bilbao: Instituto de Estudios sobre Desarrollo y Cooperación Internacional.
Hurtig, Anna Karin, and Miguel San Sebastián. 2002a. "Gynecologic and Breast Malignancies in the Amazon Basin of Ecuador, 1985–1998." *International Journal of Gynecology & Obstetrics* 76 (2): 199–201. https://doi.org/10.1016/S0020-7292(01)00546-X.
Hurtig, Anna Karin, and Miguel San Sebastián. 2002b. "Geographical Differences in Cancer Incidence in the Amazon Basin of Ecuador in Relation to Residence near Oil Fields." *International Journal of Epidemiology* 31 (5): 1021–1027. https://doi.org/10.1093/ije/31.5.1021.
Hurtig, Anna Karin, and Miguel San Sebastián. 2004a. *Cáncer en la amazonía del Ecuador (1985–1998)*. Coca, Ecuador: CICAME.
Hurtig, Anna Karin, and Miguel San Sebastián. 2004b. "Incidence of Childhood Leukemia and Oil Exploitation in the Amazon Basin of Ecuador." *International Journal of Occupational and Environmental Health* 10 (3): 245–250. https://doi.org/10.1179/oeh.2004.10.3.245.
Hurtig, Anna Karin, and Miguel San Sebastián. 2005. "Epidemiology vs Epidemiology: The Case of Oil Exploitation in the Amazon Basin of Ecuador." *International Journal of Epidemiology* 34 (5): 1170–1172. https://doi.org/10.1093/ije/dyi151.
San Sebastián, Miguel. 2000. *Informe yana curi: Impacto de la actividad petrolera en la salud de poblaciones rurales de la Amazonia ecuatoriana*. Quito: CICAME and Abya-Yala.
San Sebastián, Miguel, B. Armstrong, J. A. Córdoba, and C. Stephens. 2001. "Exposures and Cancer Incidence near Oil Fields in the Amazon Basin of Ecuador." *Occupational and Environmental Medicine* 58 (8): 517–522. https://doi.org/10.1136/oem.58.8.517.
San Sebastián, Miguel, Ben Armstrong, and Carolyn Stephens. 2002. "Outcomes of Pregnancy among Women Living in the Proximity of Oil Fields in the Amazon Basin of Ecuador." *International Journal of Occupational and Environmental Health* 8 (4): 312–319. https://pubmed.ncbi.nlm.nih.gov/12412848/.
San Sebastián, Miguel, and Anna Karin Hurtig. 2004a. "Oil Exploitation in the Amazon Basin of Ecuador: A Public Health Emergency." *Revista Panamericana de Salud Pública* 15 (3): 205–211. https://pubmed.ncbi.nlm.nih.gov/15096294/.
San Sebastián, Miguel, and Anna Karin Hurtig. 2004b. "Cancer among Indigenous People in the Amazon Basin of Ecuador, 1985–2000." *Revista Panamericana de Salud Pública* 16 (5): 328–333. https://pubmed.ncbi.nlm.nih.gov/15729982/.

San Sebastián, Miguel, and Anna Karin Hurtig. 2005. "Oil Development and Health in the Amazon Basin of Ecuador: The Popular Epidemiology Process." *Social Science & Medicine* 60 (4): 799–807. https://doi.org/10.1016/j.socscimed.2004.06.016.
Solíz Torres, María Fernanda, Pamela Cepeda Vélez, and Adolfo Maldonado Campos. 2019. *En tiempos de petróleo: Salud psicosocial en niños, niñas y adolescentes de las comunidades en las que operó Texaco*. Quito: Clinica Ambiental.
UDAPT. 2016. "Sabías qué… Informe de salud." Union de Afectados y Afectadas por las Operaciones Petroleras de Texaco. https://www.clinicambiental.org/wp-content/uploads/docs/publicaciones/informe_salud_tex.pdf.

Notes

Page Notes

The description of Lago Agrio on page 6 is adapted from *Ecuador and the Galapagos Islands* guidebook published by Lonely Planet, 2012 edition.

The image on the wall of the restaurant on page 156 is inspired by Oswaldo Guayasamin's "La Ternura" (1989).

A more complete list of the chemicals used in the various steps of the extractive process can be found in Maldonado and Narváez's *Ecuador ni es, ni será ya país amazónico: Inventario de impactos petroleros* (2003).

Notes on Type

The typeface used throughout the graphic novel is a digital version of Jonas Fischer's handwriting, meticulously crafted and brought to life by Leo Sell, who also worked on typesetting, putting to use a custom InDesign script by Joscha Brüning.

Editors: Sherine Hamdy (University of California, Irvine) and Marc Parenteau (cartoonist)

This groundbreaking series realizes ethnographic research in graphic novel form. The series speaks to a growing interest in comics as a powerful narrative medium and to the desire for a more creative and collaborative anthropology that engages the public with contemporary issues. Books in the series are informed by scholarship and combine text and image in ways that are accessible, open-ended, aesthetically rich, and that foster greater cross-cultural understanding.

Other Books in the Series

Forecasts: A Story of Weather and Finance at the Edge of Disaster, written by Caroline E. Schuster, illustrated by Enrique Bernardou and David Bueno (2023)

Messages from Ukraine, written by Gregg Bucken-Knapp, illustrated by Joonas Sildre (2022)

The King of Bangkok, written by Claudio Sopranzetti, illustrated by Sara Fabbri, adapted by Chiara Natalucci (2021)

Light in Dark Times: The Human Search for Meaning, written by Alisse Waterston and illustrated by Charlotte Corden (2020)

Gringo Love: Stories of Sex Tourism in Brazil, written by Marie-Eve Carrier-Moisan, adapted by William Flynn, illustrated by Débora Santos (2020)

Things That Art: A Graphic Menagerie of Enchanting Curiosity, written and illustrated by Lochlann Jain (2019)

Lissa: A Story about Medical Promise, Friendship, and Revolution, written by Sherine Hamdy and Coleman Nye, illustrated by Sarula Bao and Caroline Brewer, lettering by Marc Parenteau (2017)